THE BRITISH AIRMAN
OF THE
FIRST WORLD WAR

David Hadaway
with Stuart Hadaway

SHIRE PUBLICATIONS

Published in Great Britain in 2014 by Shire Publications Ltd, PO Box 883, Oxford, OX1 9PL, UK.

PO Box 3985, New York, NY 10185-3985, USA.

E-mail: shire@shirebooks.co.uk www.shirebooks.co.uk

A CIP catalogue record for this book is available from the British Library.

Shire Library no. 791. ISBN-13: 978 0 74781 368 2

David Hadaway and Stuart Hadaway have asserted their rights under the Copyright, Designs and Patents Act, 1988, to be identified as the authors of this book.

Designed by Tony Trucott Designs, Sussex, UK and typeset in Perpetua and Gill Sans.

Cover design and photography by Peter Ashley, with thanks to The Shuttleworth Collection at Old Warden, Bedfordshire; back cover: early RAF roundel.

Printed in China through Worldprint Ltd.

14 15 16 17 18   10 9 8 7 6 5 4 3 2 1

TITLE PAGE IMAGE
Major James 'Jimmy' McCudden, VC, DSO, MC, MM (see page 11–12), a leader who thought about his work, said 'If I were attacked at my disadvantage, I usually broke off the combat' and 'I think that the correct way to wage war is to down as many as possible of the enemy at the least risk, expense and casualties to one's own self'.

CONTENTS PAGE IMAGE
An SE5a and an Albatros dogfighting.

ACKNOWLEDGEMENTS
I would like to thank my wife Pip for her endless patience, my grandson Thomas for his computer tuition, and the ever-helpful staff of Stow Maries Aerodrome and the Shuttleworth Collection for their knowledge and permission to use photographs taken at their sites. This work is dedicated to my five grandchildren and three step-grandchildren, all of whom are busy with their shopping lists in anticipation of the royalties cheque.

IMAGE ACKNOWLEDGEMENTS
Bridgeman Art Library, page 4; Getty Images, page 16; Peter Cox, pages 11 (bottom), 37 and 63; Alexander Eckert, page 45; Imperial War Museum, title page and pages 6 (bottom), 10, 14, 20, 21 (top), 23 (bottom), 24 (both), 26 (top), 27 (bottom), 28 (bottom), 30 (bottom), 33, 34–5, 38, 42, 43, 48–9, 50, 53 (bottom), 58, 59 and 60; Science and Society Picture Library, page 12 (bottom); Shuttleworth Collection, pages 3, 11 (top), 36, 40, 41, 47 and 63; Stow Maries First World War Airfield, pages 30 (top) and 32; Vernon Creek, page 18.

Other images belong to the author.

CONTENTS

IN THE BEGINNING 4

THE MAKING OF AN AIRMAN 8

THE OPERATIONAL AIRMAN 16

LIFE AND DEATH IN THE AIR 38

AROUND THE WORLD 46

ON THE GROUND 54

FURTHER READING 62

PLACES TO VISIT 63

INDEX 64

BRITAIN'S NEW FLYING SERVICES

Special Pictures of the New Uniforms Worn by the Naval and Military Air Services.

DRAWN BY CHRISTOPHER CLARK FROM A SKETCH BY G. H. DAVIS

THE NEW NAVAL AIR-SERVICE UNIFORMS

IN THE BEGINNING

FROM THE HORROR of endless trenches, mud, barbed wire, machine guns and slaughter on an industrial scale there arose, literally, new heroes. Suddenly the 'knights of the air' with their 'code of chivalry' not only provided a spectator sport for the mud-caked soldiers in their trenches but were just the antidote that the public craved amidst endless casualty lists and shortages. The politicians and newspapers were quick to adopt them for their own purposes – especially the most successful and charismatic who came to be highly decorated and known as 'the Aces'. But by 1918 they were just the tip of a very large iceberg.

On 17 December 1903, just eleven years prior to the outbreak of the First World War in August 1914, the Wright brothers first flew a powered, man-carrying, heavier-than-air machine. The aeroplane was born. Interest spread worldwide and the public became fascinated by airmen, who were mostly private individuals of means, employing skilled mechanics to keep machines with temperamental engines serviceable. Some of these men became household names for their pioneering spirit and courage, and several established aircraft manufacturing companies of world repute. They wrote the text books, often based on hard-earned experience.

With varying degrees of enthusiasm the leading nations of Europe established air arms, usually supplementing lighter-than-air airships, balloons and man-lifting kites with aeroplanes. The aim was to 'see over the hill' – the reconnaissance which was the traditional role of the cavalry. Many senior officers greeted the idea of aeroplanes with distrust bordering on disgust. The Chief of the Imperial General Staff deemed aeroplanes 'a useless and expensive fad' in 1910 and the First Sea Lord thought the 'Naval requirement for aircraft was two'.

From this inauspicious start there followed two years of half-hearted organisation and reorganisation until the Royal Flying Corps (RFC) was formed in April 1912. This comprised a Military Wing, a Naval Wing and the Central Flying School (CFS). Disagreements between the army and navy led

Opposite:
Throughout the war the Royal Navy Air Service clung to its naval identity.

A war postcard which illustrates the early markings used for British aeroplanes. Unfortunately they resembled the German Maltese/Iron Cross and led to 'friendly fire' incidents. A roundel similar to that of the French was adopted but with the colours reversed.

They call us "THE EYES OF THE ARMY"
for we scout for the foe far and wide.
And with all information worth having
We keep the powers fully supplied –
There are Corps who bear much longer records
for brave deeds, yet History will find
That in the great fight
for the cause of the right.
OUR AIRMEN were not FAR BEHIND.

FROM ONE OF THE R.F.C.

Charles Samson, one of the greatest Royal Naval pilots, taking off from the forecastle of HMS *Hibernia* on 2 May 1912 – a world first. (IWM Q71041)

to the two wings parting company very quickly. By the time Britain declared war on Germany on 4 August 1914, the RFC was effectively the Military Wing and the CFS under General Sir David Henderson, while the Naval Wing had split off to become the Royal Naval Air Service, or RNAS (said by detractors to stand for Really Not A Sailor), under Captain Murray Sueter.

The RNAS was given control of all lighter-than-air aircraft (except kite balloons for artillery spotting), and defence of the homeland and coastal waters. By this time RNAS pilots had taken off from water and ships, both moored and under way, and developed the air-dropped torpedo.

On 13 August Henderson began deployment to France. Nos. 2, 3, 4 and 5 Squadrons, each nominally of twelve aeroplanes of varied makes, twenty-four officers (pilots and observers) and 130 other ranks, staged through Dover, Kent, en route to Amiens, France. Their ground equipment was transported in assorted vehicles requisitioned from private companies without time for them to be repainted, presenting a colourful sight. No. 5 Squadron's equipment travelled in a large red van with 'Bovril' emblazoned on the sides.

The first wave included the commanding officers of No. 2 Squadron, Major C. J. B. 'Pregnant Percy' Burke, and of No. 5 Squadron, the monocled Major J. F. A. 'All bum and eye glass' Higgins. Each aircraft carried a mechanic in the front cockpit in lieu of an observer. The honour of being the first to land in France went to Lieutenant H. D. 'H-K' Harvey-Kelly,

Lt 'Reggie' Marix, DSO, RN at a temporary airfield in 1914. He flew in the bombing raids on Germany on 21 September 1914 and successfully on 8 October.

who incurred the considerable wrath of Major Burke by cutting a corner and thwarting the latter's desire to be the first!

Lieutenant Louis Strange of No. 5 Squadron had an unwilling and terrified passenger who fortified himself en route with a bottle of whisky. At Dover he was placed under arrest but escaped into the town for more of the same. Strange hunted him down, and on arrival at Amiens the man received fifty-six days' field punishment.

By 19 August 1914 the RFC had commenced aerial reconnaissance patrols and is acknowledged with saving the army from possible annihilation at Mons with timely reports of the German movements. By 22 October the RNAS launched a bombing raid on Zeppelin sheds in Cologne and Dusseldorf, but was thwarted by the weather.

1914...
Ce qui reste d'un avion allemand descendu aux environs de Villers-Coterets | What is left of a german aeroplane brought down near Villers-Coterets

In late 1914 a crashed enemy aircraft was enough of a novelty to warrant the printing of a bilingual postcard.

THE MAKING OF AN AIRMAN

The young airman lay dying
Amidst the wreckage he lay
To the mechanics who 'round him came sighing
These last parting words he did say:
'Take the cylinders out of my kidneys,
The connecting rods out of my brain:
The crankshaft out of my backbone,
And assemble the engine again.'
(To the tune of 'Tarpaulin Jacket')

THE FLYING SERVICES recruited from throughout the army and navy, as well as from the civilian population. New entrants could volunteer at the age of seventeen, with aircrew applicants joining sometimes straight from school, although they would not be called up until the age of eighteen. Once in, early pilot training was variable. There was the CFS at Upavon on Salisbury Plain, whilst the independently minded RNAS also had their Naval Flying School (NFS) at Eastchurch in Kent. After ground instruction at one of the Schools of Aeronautics, entrants were usually trained to fly at a private flying school, followed by military flying training at CFS or NFS. However, the latter two struggled to accommodate the expansion that followed the dawning realisation amongst senior officers of the value of an air arm, and soon more service flying schools were established across the country. Apart from flying training, new aeroplane pilot entrants usually only received the most basic of military training. RNAS candidates received just one week of instruction in Royal Navy traditions, discipline and administration. Applicants could also transfer from elsewhere in the army or navy. Those joining the RFC from other units kept their regimental uniforms (including kilts) with the addition of pilots' 'wings' on their chests. Direct entrants wore the famous double-breasted 'maternity jacket'.

Opposite:
A trainee aircrew officer, with his white cap flash, 'maternity jacket', swagger stick and the gloves that no officer would 'walk out' without.

9

Flying training was also very basic to begin with, as were the aircraft used. The Caudron G3 was a French design, very front-heavy and dangerously under-powered, with a nacelle suspended between the wings. One pupil described it as follows:

> A nacelle was rather like a wooden bath that you sat in and the engine was stuck in front of you. There were open booms to the tail rather than a fuselage. You only had 35 horse-power and we used to say that if one horse died, you did too. In fact the stall point and the maximum speed were very nearly the same.

Maurice Farman 'Longhorns' were also common training aircraft. Cedric Hill recalled:

> There was no dual control fitted on the Longhorns. There were two seats in tandem. The instructor sat in the front seat and the petrified pupil in the back, holding the controls with the instructor by leaning forward underneath his arms. It was impossible for the pupil to get his feet near the rudder bar.

At the time flying was very dependent on the weather – winds that were too strong, especially a crosswind, 'bumpy' air (turbulence) or poor visibility ruled out flying. Instructors usually made a trial flight to 'test the weather' or possibly puffed on a cigarette to judge the wind's strength and direction.

A pilot precariously perched in a Caudron G3. This one has a camera attached to the back of the nacelle for taking photographs of the ground. (IWM HU 91040)

Airmen came from many backgrounds. Louis Strange was a farmer who, after being kicked by a sheep and left unable to work, decided to learn to fly at Hendon. It took him three weeks to complete the three-and-a-half hours' flying needed for his 'ticket' (a Royal Aero Club Pilot's Certificate), which he was awarded in August 1913. Claude Graham-White, flying-school owner and aircraft manufacturer, recognised his talent and offered him employment. Strange gave flying tuition, participated in air races (organised to stretch men and machines, often for prizes and trophies) and undertook joy flights. In early 1914 he applied to join the RFC and was called to the CFS in May.

The cockpit of a BE2, showing the rudimentary nature of the instruments.

Mechanically minded 2nd Lieutenant Albert Ball of the Sherwood Foresters could drive cars and motorcycles before enlistment. In June 1915 he was sent on a platoon leaders' course in Perivale, Middlesex, 4 miles from Hendon aerodrome. He enrolled in the Ruffy-Baumann Flying School and so each day rose at 3 am, motorcycled to Hendon, took tuition and returned for the 6.45 am parade and a frequent reprimand for his appearance. It took Ball four months to obtain his 'ticket'. He then declined to be sent straight to France as an observer and was posted to No. 9 (Reserve) Squadron near Norwich, as training squadrons were then known, for further training; thence to the CFS for about one month of advanced training; and then to Gosport, Hampshire as an instructor.

'Jimmy' McCudden was a 'Barrack Rat'. The son of a Royal Engineers non-commissioned officer (NCO) serving at Gillingham, Kent, he joined

Designed by Roy Chadwick (who went on to design the Lancaster Bomber), the Avro 504K saw active service before becoming the RFC's best training aircraft. It remained in service well into the 1930s.

The most successful British 'Ace' Major Edward 'Mick' Mannock, VC, DSO, MC with seventy-three victories.

the Royal Engineers as a bugler, aged fifteen years. With his elder brother Bill he had spent time at the nearby Leysdown and Eastchurch airfields, watching the flying. Bill joined the Royal Engineers before transferring to the RFC, becoming an NCO pilot, and was killed in May 1915 whilst instructing at Fort Grange airfield, Gosport. Jimmy enrolled for Man's Service on reaching his eighteenth birthday in April 1913 and transferred to the RFC as an engine fitter. Having gone to France with No. 3 Squadron in the first RFC contingent, as a qualified 'marksman' he often flew as an observer armed with a rifle. Early applications for pilot training were turned down due to his proficiency as a mechanic; good mechanics were harder to find than pilots!

Although clearly staged for the camera, this photograph gives a good impression of the inside of a barrack hut for other ranks.

After accumulating one hundred hours airborne, promotion to sergeant, the award of the Croix de Guerre from French General Joffre, and an

observer's half-wing brevet, his persistence succeeded and he was posted to his brother's old training squadron at Fort Grange. After four hours' instruction he flew solo and passed his Royal Aero Club (RAeC) test the same day. After a few days at the CFS for advanced training he was sent as an instructor to nearby Netheravon with nine hours fifteen minutes in his log book. Three weeks later the total was seventy-four hours. In July he began his active service flying FE2bs with No. 20 Squadron. In August he transferred to No. 29 Squadron, flying DH2 single-seat Scouts, winning the Military Medal (MM) and soon afterwards he was commissioned and awarded the Military Cross (MC).

Like his great friend Jimmy McCudden, Edward 'Mick' Mannock was a 'Barrack Rat'. When war broke out he was working in Turkey. He was interned and badly treated before being repatriated in the belief that he was blind in one eye. He certainly had problems with the sight in his left eye but he joined the Royal Army Medical Corps (RAMC). He transferred to the Royal Engineers and was commissioned before applying to the RFC, somehow disguising his sight defect. His training followed the usual path except that his instructor at No. 10 (Reserve) Squadron was Jimmy McCudden on a rest from France.

Reginald 'Rex' Warneford, a merchant navy officer, joined the army in January 1915. One month later he transferred to the RNAS and was sent to a civilian flying school at Hendon. He obtained his RAeC certificate in two weeks and spent a short time at CFS Upavon before undertaking advanced training at NFS Eastchurch. The RNAS, with responsibility for home defence, was under pressure due to Zeppelin airships bombing Britain with seeming impunity, and he was posted as a Flight Sub Lieutenant to No. 1 (Naval) Squadron at Dunkirk, France, which was tasked with combating them as they crossed the North Sea.

The Eastchurch Squadron at Dunkirk, France in 1914, showing the mixture of aircraft employed. From left to right, these aircraft are: BE2 No. 50, Commander Charles Samson's favourite aircraft; a Henry Farman F20; a Sopwith Tractor No. 42; and the airship Astra Torres No.3.

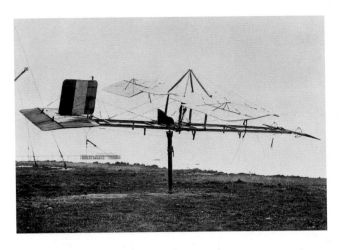

This contraption was used to test a trainee's resilience to airsickness at RNAS Lee-on-Solent – a forerunner of the modern simulator? (IWM Q 69458)

John 'Jack' Alcock left school at sixteen and became an apprentice engineer. The firm's owner also designed and built aeroplanes and Jack was encouraged to help. Later he was asked to work on an engine belonging to the owner of Brooklands Flying School, near Weybridge in Surrey. This led to flying lessons, and he became both a sought-after mechanic and successful air racer. At the outbreak of war he was pressed into service with the RNAS at Eastchurch NFS with his own aircraft as a civilian instructor. Rex Warneford was one of his graduates. In December 1916 he applied for a commission and became a Flight Lieutenant, Royal Naval Volunteer Reserve (RNVR).

The training death toll was high for both pupils and 'resting' experienced instructors. As a rough guide, 10,000 airmen died in the war: 4,000 in training, 4,000 in post-training accidents and only 2,000 as a result of enemy attacks.

The ad hoc nature of this training led to inexperienced pilots being thrown into battle with inevitable consequences. Some instructors were, as with Ball and McCudden, barely trained themselves. Others were combat pilots needing a rest, but teaching unskilled pupils did little to restore their equilibrium and it is understandable that instructors commonly referred to their pupils as 'Huns'. Fifteen hours' solo flying before posting to a squadron was the aim in 1916, but training was dependent on the war situation. A crisis arose during the 'Fokker Scourge' from July 1915 to September 1916 when Fokker *Eindeckers* (monoplanes), with forward firing guns, reaped a heavy toll. Training was cut short as the need for quantity overrode quality. Major General Hugh Trenchard, RFC commander in France, insisted on an aggressive offensive policy but also decreed that all empty chairs would be filled in the mess by the next day.

Experienced men knew that there must be a better way and this became the obsession of the outspoken Major Robert Smith-Barry. After being wounded in France, he was given command of No.1 (Reserve) Squadron at Gosport in December 1916 with the brief to put his ideas into practice. The resulting 'Gosport System' remains the basis of service flying training worldwide today.

His philosophy was that all pilots knew how to fly an aeroplane but few pilots knew *why* an aeroplane flew. He began by teaching the teachers. All training courses were to be standardised on the Avro 504, a two-seater biplane with good performance and full dual controls. The pupil in front could hear his instructor through a stethoscope device known as a 'Gosport tube', replacing thumps and gesticulations as a means of communication. Even after flying solo, the pupil would receive frequent dual instruction in a structured course to build on his experience and confidence. Instructors would allow the pupil to get into potentially dangerous situations, rather than indulge in preventive self-preservation as previously, and then teach them how to overcome them. The course rounded off with training on the aircraft which the pupil would fly in combat. Casualty rates fell dramatically.

As his courses produced results the Royal Aero Club could not keep pace with the examinations for 'tickets' and, recognising that the Smith-Barry standard was higher than their own, was prepared to issue a certificate on proof that the applicant had been 'Passed by Gosport'. Many graduates did not bother and others went straight to war and died before the paperwork caught up.

RNAS airship pilots served two months' initial general training with the Seaman's Branch which was followed by commissioning as a probationary flight sub lieutenant and a course at the Balloon Training Unit at Wormwood Scrubs, West London. Initially five pupils trained in a basket carried beneath a balloon with their instructor before soloing in a two-man airship. Kite balloon crews were trained at Roehampton, Surrey, and were part of the RFC.

An observation or kite balloon ascent, showing the labour-intensive operation as the crew clamber into the basket amongst gas cylinders and the waiting winch lorry.

THE OPERATIONAL
AIRMAN

B Y 1916 RFC brigades each comprised two wings – one for the corps (army co-operation, namely artillery-spotting and reconnaissance) and one for the Army (bombing and fighting). Each wing consisted of several squadrons, nominally of eighteen aeroplanes. Initially aircraft like the BE2 were used in a variety of roles, but by 1916 specialist aircraft and units were appearing. Each squadron was commanded by a major who was not required to fly in combat, and many did not, until the McCudden/Mannock breed of 'come on' rather than 'go on' leaders appeared. The squadron comprised of two flights, each commanded by a captain who led the fighting formations. The leaders could be identified by streamers flown from the tails or struts of their 'buses'. They would communicate their orders via Very lights (pistol flares) and hand signals.

A kite balloon wing was attached to each brigade under command of a lieutenant colonel. Each wing consisted of five or more kite balloon companies led by a major or captain and each of three or four sections. Swinging in a basket beneath a hydrogen-inflated balloon for many hours at a time, the crews were very exposed both to the elements and the enemy. If they could see the Germans then the Germans could see them and endeavour to destroy them by aircraft or artillery fire. In a crisis the two-man crews, who wore harnesses, could parachute to safety using a pack attached to the basket whilst the ground crew endeavoured to winch the balloon down before it erupted in flames (the failure rate of the parachutes was estimated at 1:1000). Not only the observers but also the ground crew suffered casualties and the crews regarded themselves as 'bal-lunatics'. Owing to the nature of their work the sections frequently moved and often lived under canvas.

It was not solely a pilots' war. The original intention of using military aircraft was and remained reconnaissance. Soon the necessity for an observer became obvious. The pilot was fully occupied just flying, especially when vulnerable to attack from enemy anti-aircraft guns and aeroplanes.

Opposite:
British and German biplanes engage in a dogfight, from the *Sphere*, October 1917.

Pilots and observers in a modern reconstruction confer over a map before a flight. Once airborne, communications were very limited.

An observer could concentrate on events below and transmit information via a dropped message, a klaxon or wireless telegraphy (WT), enabling the pilot to concentrate on keeping them alive. Lighter wireless sets and more powerful engines enabled aeroplanes which had previously struggled to take off under the weight of their crews to carry sets, and artillery spotting 'took off'. Enterprising observers originated a celluloid sheet with clock segments centred on a target and concentric rings at set distances. Overlaid on maps coordinated with the artillery, the 'Clock Code' allowed accurate reporting of the fall of shot. At the outbreak of war the observers were often trained pilots until the wastage became unsustainable and observer training schools were then set up. Pilot Major Hugh 'Stuffy' Dowding had been retained in charge of the Dover Despatch Camp but constantly badgered Trenchard for a posting to France. He got his wish – but as an observer with No. 6 Squadron!

Having experienced the difficulty of recording his observations, Lieutenant C. C. Darley began experimenting with a privately purchased camera and developing equipment. He was able to demonstrate the value of studying photographs to staff officers planning an attack, and soon each wing was equipped with a photo section and a darkroom lorry. By 1918 the RFC was taking photographs of the entire front line twice a day. These were patched together into 'photo-mosaics' that could be compared, every enemy position plotted and any changes noted. New gun batteries, trenches, supply dumps or infrastructure could indicate a coming attack, and equally any new weaknesses in the enemy defences could be identified.

Inevitably someone objected to the opposition roaming into their airspace and crews started taking potshots at each other with rifles and, later, machine guns. Soon dedicated aircraft were employed solely to see off trespassers and to protect their own machines when snooping over the other side. They became known as 'scouts', and later as 'fighters'. The British policy was to patrol scouts above German airspace, allowing their observation aircraft to fly directly above the German front lines, while the Germans and the French were less aggressive. As the prevailing winds in France are from the west, this often meant that British aircraft, near the end of their patrols or in trouble, had to fight strong headwinds to get back to the safety of their own lines.

If aircraft could enter the enemy airspace to reconnoitre then it was realised that they could also drop explosives on suitable targets. The bomber was born. On 24 April 1915 Lieutenant Willie Rhodes-Moorhouse was sent to bomb Courtrai railway junction in a BE2. In order to carry a 112-pound bomb his observer was left behind. The junction was successfully bombed from 300 feet but the BE2 and Rhodes-Moorhouse suffered severely from ground fire. On return to base Rhodes-Moorhouse insisted on making his report before accepting medical aid. He was posthumously awarded the first air Victoria Cross (VC) for this action.

Rudimentary bombsights appeared to help aeroplanes to drop bombs accurately, including one co-invented by Louis Strange, and the training in their use led to bombing schools. Aerial gunnery schools followed as

'B' Flight, RFC Artillery Co-operation School, at Lydd, Kent, in 1918.

practical aircraft machine guns and mountings for them appeared. Necessity may be the mother of invention but war is too often the mother of necessity and the early 'Jack of all trades' aeroplane gave way to specialist models.

The Royal Navy was not only busy combating Zeppelins but had responsibility for protection of shipping from submarines, and especially the troopships shuttling between Folkestone and France. Sea Scout (SS) class airships and their successors based at RN Air Station Capel le Ferne, in Kent, had the endurance to make a difference and could employ WT to summon vessels of the famed Dover Patrol to deal with sightings.

These airships were basically non-rigid gas bags (Zeppelins had a rigid framework) with the fuselage of an aircraft, less wings and tail, slung below. The rudder and pedals to control 'yaw' and an elevator wheel to control 'pitch' were retained. The BE2 was frequently used although fuselages with rear-mounted engines were preferred by the crews as being considerably less draughty. They would carry 60 gallons of fuel, 300 gallons of water ballast, a grapple and a trail rope. The pilot was assisted by an observer/ WT operator and a mechanic. With little protection from the cold, after eight-hour flights the crews often had to be lifted from the cockpits. It required 150 men to haul down an airship, especially in a wind. In April 1915

A Sea Scout Zero (SSZ) class airship was 143 feet long, with a diameter of 32 feet and a maximum speed of 53 mph. (IWM Q 27507)

Leading Mechanic William Stanford became entangled when the wind caught an airship and fell from 700 feet, breaking every bone in his body and making a two-foot indent in the ground.

There was an almost pathological fear of Zeppelin attacks amongst the British public even before the outbreak of hostilities, whipped up over several years by lurid magazine articles (like 'The Aerial Battleship' which appeared in *McClure's Magazine* in America in August 1909) or H. G. Wells's apocalyptic novel *The War in the Air*. In the first months of the war several air raids were launched by the RNAS to attack Zeppelin sheds in northern Germany. Due to the very long ranges involved, the aircraft often flew from or via airfields in France or Belgium, but Christmas Day 1914 saw a world's first for British airmen, with a strike being flown from the sea.

The Harwich Naval Force led a seaborne attack against the Cuxhaven Zeppelin Base on the German North Sea coast. Amongst the warships were

A Zeppelin was the length of two football pitches and could carry two tons of bombs at 50 to 65 mph. The main defensive aeroplane, the BE2, was slightly longer than the width of a goalmouth. (IWM Q 58481)

'Take cover.' The concept of policemen on bicycles blowing whistles with placards around their necks may seem comic, but to the unprepared public the concept of air raids was anything but funny, and the total lack of experience of them led to desperate measures.

three ex-South Eastern and Chatham Railway's Cross-Channel ferries, each with three Short two-seater seaplanes to be lowered onto the water and each capable of carrying three Hales 20-pound bombs. Pilots were given

The cover of *McClure's Magazine*, August 1909, typical of the popular and lurid articles which helped fuel fears of aerial attacks before the war.

THE FLIGHT OF THE "WILD DUCKS": THE START OF THE GREAT NAVAL AIR RAID ON THE ZEEBRUGGE DISTRICT.

EXCEEDING IN MAGNITUDE ANY PREVIOUS EXPOSITION OF AERIAL WARFARE: DEPARTURE OF THE "THIRTY-FOUR NAVAL AEROPLANES AND SEAPLANES" FOR THEIR SUCCESSFUL RAID ON GERMAN SUBMARINE BASES IN BELGIUM.

The Illustrated London News's exaggerated interpretation of the raid by thirty-four aeroplanes on Zeebrugge, Belgium, on 12 February 1915. The official history states that only twelve land fighters and one seaplane were involved, although several targets on the Belgian coast were hit.

Airshiplane Number 1. RNAS Wing Commander N. F. Usborne and Squadron Commander D. W. P. Ireland's innovative attempt to quickly gain the altitude necessary to combat Zeppelins led to their deaths, when the front wires broke away and they were tipped out. (IWM Q73629)

the option of carrying observers; four did and one observer was author Lieutenant Robert Erskine Childers, RNVR, who helped plan the raid. The force was hampered by thick fog and the operation failed as an air/surface battle developed. Some seaplanes were shot down but the crews were recovered by ships or submarines.

The first Zeppelin raid on Britain was not until 19/20 January 1915 when two Zeppelins bombed Great Yarmouth and Sheringham in Norfolk, killing three people. From April the night-time raids increased and casualties and damage mounted. Defending aircraft struggled to reach the altitude

Morane-Saulnier Type L Parasol Monoplane No. 3253, flown by Flight Sub Lieutenant 'Rex' Warneford when he downed Zeppelin LZ37. The British needed more aeroplanes than the Royal Aircraft Factory could provide, so it was necessary to acquire French aircraft, which were often superior in any case. The British authorities had decided that monoplanes were inherently dangerous and had banned their manufacture. (IWM HU 67827)

necessary to attack the Zeppelins, even supposing their position could be detected in the dark.

This all changed on 7 June 1915. Flight Sub Lieutenant Rex Warneford, flying a French Morane-Saulnier Type L Monoplane, loaded with six 20-pound Hales bombs but no gun, intercepted Zeppelin LZ37 near Ostend, Belgium, as it returned from an aborted raid on London. High winds and fog had caused the mission to be cancelled but wireless intercepts alerted the pilots at St Pol aerodrome, in France. After a twenty-minute duel with the Zeppelin defending itself robustly, Warneford succeeded in gaining the height necessary to bomb the airship, which crashed in flames

Warneford (far right) and other successful anti-Zeppelin pilots: J. S. Mills (far left) and J. P. Wilson (third left) who destroyed Zeppelin LZ38 in her shed at Evere on 7 June 1915 and A. W. Bigsworth, DSO, who severely damaged LZ39 over Ostend on the same night that Warneford destroyed LZ37. (IWM Q 69479)

onto a convent in Ghent. The explosion inverted his aeroplane, stopping the engine. He landed behind enemy lines, repaired his engine and flew back to base. He was awarded the Victoria Cross but was killed ten days later trialling a new French-designed aircraft.

The RNAS also established coastal seaplane stations flying two-seater aeroplanes carrying a mechanic, a necessity should they be forced to 'land' on the sea with engine failure. In dire circumstances rescue usually depended on the aircraft's carrier pigeons summoning help from a ship contacted by their base. The Chatham Naval Memorial commemorates the many sailors who died during the First World War with no known graves, most of whom perished at sea.

By 1917 long-range flying boats such as the Felixstowe F2A, with a crew of four equipped with seven Lewis guns and about 500-pound bomb loads, were in service. It was not uncommon for RNAS seaplanes and land fighters to go into combat with their German equivalents over the North Sea, with a watery fate for the vanquished. A variety of life jackets were evolving; some employed buoyant kapok and others required a bladder to be inflated. Early pilots flying the English Channel were issued with tyre inner tubes.

The crews devised the 'Spider's Web' to aid in searching for German submarines ('*Unterseebooten*' or 'U-boats'). It involved an octagon centred on the North Hilder Lightship with 30 mile-long radial arms. Two segments could be covered by each aircraft patrol with the possibility of redirection to a suspected U-boat. Five-hour-long patrols were very demanding for the crews and especially for the pilot who had no hydraulics or trimming devices

The Chatham Naval Memorial to sailors with no known grave includes 105 members of the RNAS who served aboard ships that had Chatham as their home base. Similar memorials exist at Plymouth and Portsmouth.

Right: A Felixstowe F3 being recovered ashore in Malta in 1918. The boats were built in the dockyard there and needed around thirty men to haul them from the water. (IWM Q 27456)

Below: Seaplane carrier HMS *Ben-my-Chree* was originally an Isle of Man Steam Packet Company vessel. She was converted with a large hangar aft and derricks to lift her complement of up to six Short 184 seaplanes onto and off the water.

Left: A Felixstowe
F2A flying boat,
capable of an
eight-hour patrol
over the North Sea.
(IWM Q 27501)

A pilot's-eye view from a Sopwith Pup.

Church parade at No. 2 Aeroplane Supply Depot. A 'Fee' cockpit makes a useful and appropriate pulpit for the padre in September 1918. (IWM 12110)

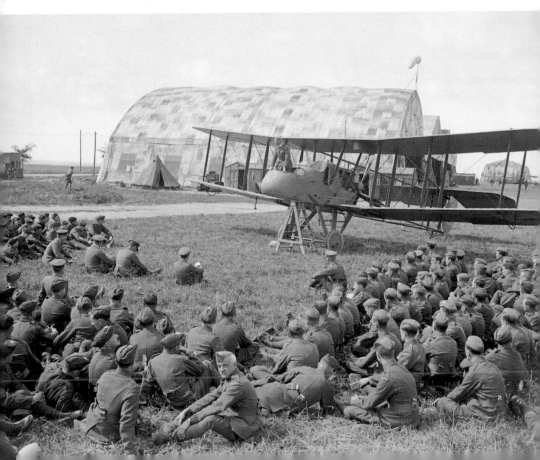

to relieve the strain on his arms. Just staring at the sea, the cold and engine noise took their toll, resulting in frozen, deafened and exhausted crews.

The ground crews who launched flying boats (whose hulls sat in the water) and seaplanes (which relied on floats to keep theirs out of it) pushed trolleys down slipways into the sea. Equipped with armpit-length waders and weighted boots, they also suffered from the cold and a lost footing in rough seas was often fatal.

The Western Front air war developed a nip-and-tuck routine with each side gaining supremacy until a new aeroplane or fresh tactic countered it. The problem of firing a machine gun forward without hitting the propeller occupied Louis Strange from the first. He mounted a Lewis machine gun alongside his cockpit angled to fire outside the propeller arc. It proved impractical to fly in one direction and fire in another. A French solution fitted metal plates to the propeller blades to deflect any bullets striking it. The Germans

The Bystander. October 18, 1916

135

The Height of Impudence

FRITZ (from the basket of Zeppelin): "I say, old man, could you let me have a copper? Our gas is running out!"

The Bystander's attitude to Zeppelins, demonstrating the established British trait of poking fun in adversity.

quickly enrolled Dutch aircraft designer Anthony Fokker to better it and he devised an interrupter gear which stopped the gun firing when the propeller blade was in the way. Once fitted to his nimble new monoplane (known as an *Eindecker*) the 'Fokker Scourge' began. From July 1915 through the Somme Battle period until September 1916 the Allied airmen suffered.

The British countered with single- and two-seater pusher aeroplanes. The two-seater FE2b 'Fee' (a Geoffrey de Havilland design) was equipped with one Lewis gun mounted to be fired forward by the front cockpit observer, with another mounted to fire rearwards over the top wing – not so easy standing up with little restraint when travelling erratically at over 70 mph. The primary role remained reconnaissance but pusher crews now

A timely warning?
(Stow Maries
aerodrome)

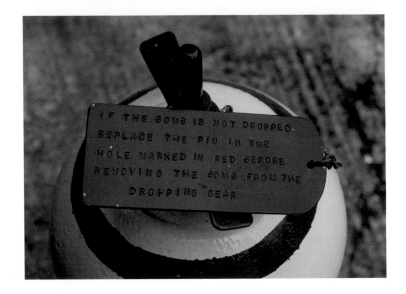

had a fighting chance over those still flying any of the 'Stability Jane' BE2 variants, also known as 'Quirks' to the RFC pilots that were forced to fly and die in them long after they were obsolete. Stability was fine for taking photographs or studying the ground below but self-defence was severely

Bomb damage in Long Acre, Central London, 28/29 January 1918. In the worst bombing incident of the war thirty-eight people died and ninety were injured when a 300 kg bomb penetrated to a shelter under Odhams Press. (IWM HO122A)

hampered by that very stability. A clear view of an aggressor with the ability to take instant avoiding action and self-defence was more appreciated by the crews.

The Martinsyde S1 Scout mounted a drum-fed Lewis gun above the top wing. Captain Louis Strange quickly commandeered one of the first to reach No. 6 Squadron. In May 1915 he was scrapping with a German Aviatik two-seater reconnaissance aeroplane when he needed to replace his ammunition drum only to find it had jammed. To free it he stood, holding the control stick between his knees whilst he struggled to free the drum. Perhaps inevitably his knees slipped and the aircraft inverted, tipping Strange out until he was only hanging onto the drum. Somehow he managed to transfer his grip to the wing and kick the control column to right his 'bus' and drop back into his 'office'. His fellow flight commander Captain Lanoe Hawker was to win the VC flying a DH2 pusher (known as 'the Flying Incinerator') but later lost his life fighting a duel with Manfred von Richthofen – the 'Red Baron' and the highest-scoring Ace of either side.

At home the day of the Zeppelins ended in September 1916 when Lieutenant William 'Robbie' Leefe Robinson earned the Victoria Cross for shooting down Zeppelin SL11 over Cuffley, Hertfordshire, in a BE2c equipped with new incendiary/explosive ammunition mix. The spectre of the burning Zeppelin routed the fifteen other airships en route to attack London. By the end of the year four more Zeppelins had been shot down.

The Zeppelins were withdrawn to be replaced by Gotha twin-engine bombers. The problem of detection persisted and at times crack squadrons

On 3 September 1916 Lieutenant William Leefe-Robinson of No. 39 Squadron took off from Suttons Farm (later renamed Hornchurch) aerodrome in a BE2c and downed Zeppelin SL11. This was not a true naval Zeppelin with an aluminium framework but a wooden-framed army 'Schütte-Lanz', no less hard to destroy.

The well-preserved First World War Stow Maries Aerodrome in Essex from where home defence patrols flew day and night.

were withdrawn from the Western Front to boost the home defence squadrons before Gotha losses led to their withdrawal. Just prior to Leefe-Robinson's success, the 'B' flight commander of his No. 39 Squadron was Captain Arthur Harris, known to his friends as 'Bert' and later to the public as 'Bomber' and to his Bomber Command crews as 'Butch'.

From necessity home defence was frequently conducted at night. In the absence of flying instruments considered as basic today, airfield landing aids consisted of burning pots of fuel-soaked rags arranged in an 'L' shape, and with no airfield control tower or wireless air-to-ground communications, casualties were high. On 31 January 1916 fifteen aircraft took off from various airfields chasing Zeppelins. Thirteen were damaged to varying degrees and three pilots were killed, principally as a result of attempts to land in the dark. Forced landing away from an airfield was even more dangerous.

Interception was complicated because frequently the Zeppelins, unsure of their position, wandered erratically looking for a target to bomb. Later co-operation between searchlights, anti-aircraft guns and the patrolling pilots brought dividends but successful interception remained problematical.

Flying was always fraught and at the mercy of weather, engine and structural failure, together with barely suitable landing grounds. Lieutenant L. L. 'Air Hog' Morgan, MC (whose nickname reflected his constant desire to be airborne) had lost his right leg when his Nieuport 23 Scout was hit by friendly fire over France. He then flew with No. 50 (Home Defence) Squadron from Bekesbourne airfield, Kent, with a wooden leg that he dubbed 'Prudence'. Taking off on 26 April 1918, the engine of his SE5 cut out and, confronted with a high railway embankment, he stalled attempting to return. The aircraft crashed and Morgan was killed.

4-Engine Handley Page — showing Rolls-Royce Engines.

The massive
Handley Page
V/1500.

In France the lumbering BE2s had been surpassed by better bomb carriers. The FE2s which had helped defeat the Fokker *Eindeckers* were soon themselves outclassed and were reborn as day and night bombers and later as night fighters. They were reinforced by Airco DH4s and DH9s (Geoffrey de Havilland again) and the huge Handley Page bombers commonly called the 'Bloody Paralysers' of the RNAS. The RNAS led the way with large-scale bombing raids. In early 1915 thirty-five- to forty-strong formations were attacking railway communications and strategic targets in occupied areas.

The Handley Page 0/100 and 0/400 saw much service as long-range bombers, although their big brother the V/1500 was too late to accomplish its intended role – bombing Berlin. Compared to the frail, low-powered machines of only a few years before, these were massive and solid aircraft. The wingspan of the 0/100 and 0/400 was 100 feet for the upper wings and 70 feet for the lower, and the crew of three was accommodated in a fuselage over 60 feet long. They typically carried sixteen 112-pound bombs with four or five Lewis guns for protection, while the largest bomb dropped by a 0/400 weighed 1,650 pounds (see table below).

No example of the giant V/1500 remains, but here for comparison is the size against aircraft that can be seen in museums.

	V/1500	Vickers Vimy	Avro Lancaster	Avro Vulcan
Wingspan	126 feet	68 feet	102 feet	111 feet
Length	64 feet	43 feet	69 feet 6 inches	100 feet
Height	23 feet	15 feet 7 ½ inches	20 feet	27 feet

Flight Lieutenant John Alcock, DSC, in a Maurice Farman Longhorn before the outbreak of war (IWM Q 66120).

Flight Lieutenant John Alcock, DSC, took off on 30 September 1917 to bomb Istanbul, then known as Constantinople. His Handley Page 0/100 was loaded with twenty 112-pound bombs and twelve incendiary bombs. Damage from anti-aircraft fire over Gallipoli resulted in a forced landing in the sea and he became a prisoner of the Turks. On the 14/15 June 1919, seven months after his release, he and RAF pilot Captain Arthur Whitten Brown became the first to fly the Atlantic in a converted Vickers Vimy bomber. They were knighted but on 18 December 1919 Sir John Alcock was killed in a flying accident.

Scout aircraft continued to get faster, more rugged and more powerful. Sopwith 1½ Strutters, Pups, Camels and Snipes fought alongside SE5a aircraft, Bristol Scouts and the peerless two-seater Bristol F2b fighters ('Biffs' or 'Brisfits'). The RNAS, who held the coastal end of the front, flew the Sopwith Triplane – 'Tripehound' or simply 'Tripes' – which compensated for lack of speed with the ability to 'climb like a homesick angel and turn on a sixpence'. Common cruising speeds were in the vicinity of 100 mph with the ability to reach over 180 mph in a dive. The speed and manoeuvrability of the aircraft led to their combats becoming known as 'dogfights', as the aircraft swirled around. James McCudden recalled the large dogfights of 1917 and 1918:

I really feel at a loss to describe some of these enormous formation fights which took place daily. About thirty machines would all be mixed up together, and viewed from a distance it seemed as if a swarm of bees were all circling around a honey-pot. Then perhaps one would notice a little speck start to go down, a trickle of flame would start behind it, and then grow larger, until the machine looked like a comet diving earthwards, leaving a long trail of black smoke to mark its line of fall.

The Bristol F2b two-seater fighter – the 'Biff' or later the 'Brisfit' – was an excellent aircraft which remained in service into the 1930s.

Sopwith Triplanes were relatively slow but highly manoeuvrable with an impressive rate of climb. The all-Canadian 'Black Flight' of No. 10 Naval Squadron, led by sixty-victory 'Ace' Raymond Collishaw, were especially effective. He made six claims in one day flying a 'Tripe'.

Following pages: A posed photograph of a 22 Squadron Bristol fighter, crews and mechanics (IWM Q 11992).

LIFE AND DEATH
IN THE AIR

A S THE SPEEDS, ceilings, endurance and structural strength to sustain violent manoeuvres increased, so did the physical demands on the crews. Just as importantly, the psychological strain suffered became recognised. Apart from enemy machines and 'Archie' (as anti-aircraft fire was known, from a music-hall song), the very real possibility of mechanical failure, the cold and lack of oxygen at altitude all took their toll. With each extra 1,000 feet of altitude the temperature dropped by two degrees centigrade. Cockpits were bare and open. Although flying kit was issued to other ranks as necessary, for much of the war warm clothing for officers had to be privately purchased from an outfitter such as Gieves, although Scottish Captain 'Bruce' Prothero insisted on flying in a kilt. When asked why, he explained that he did not want to be shot down and taken prisoner when improperly dressed. Long leather coats were the norm until Flight Sub Lieutenant Sidney Cotton invented a one-piece 'Sidcot' flying suit which remained in issue throughout the Second World War. Leather, sheepskin-lined gloves and even face masks all helped to give some protection from the elements.

Faces could also be smeared with whale grease, and a silk scarf was not so much a fashion accessory but a necessity to clean goggles with – rotary engines sprayed out castor oil at two gallons per hour. Apocryphal stories exist of constipated airmen running behind taxiing machines, breathing the fumes in deeply. A pilot who failed to see an enemy creeping up would be unlikely to need a laxative.

Flying helmets were not standardised but usually consisted of a soft leather cap lined with chamois leather and insulated with fur or cloth and silk. Various designs appeared but none gave any real protection in a crash. Rudimentary oxygen masks began to appear for high-flying bomber crews, as did electrically heated flying suits, but were not general issue.

The term 'Ace' to denote someone with five or more victories was copied from the French and not widely known amongst the squadrons until

Opposite:
One of the few aircrew NCOs, Flight Sergeant W. G. Bennett, illustrating his protective clothing. He was wounded in the leg by groundfire while flying a contact patrol in a BE2a with No. 15 Squadron on 4 May 1917 during the Battle of Arras. April 1917 saw the bulk of the Battle of Arras and went down in RFC/RAF history as 'Bloody April' due to the extremely high losses suffered. A contact patrol overflew a battle and attempted to plot the position of the opposing armies. (IWM ART 2397)

A re-enactor dressed in full flying kit against the freezing temperatures of high-level flight.

the press grasped it. The official policy was to publicise the actions of the British Aces but, with few exceptions such as Ball, keep their identities from the public. The French and Germans treated theirs like superstars.

Albert Ball, who flew bareheaded, was highly strung and very successful. Although he did not shun life in the mess he built himself a hut on the airfield where he lived alone and grew vegetables. In the evenings he would light a red flare imbedded in the ground and walk around it, playing his violin. Signs of his deterioration were there to see: he became sullen and bad-tempered and increasingly tired; he shook and yawned without control and ranted that the Germans were all cowards. On 7 May 1917 he became separated in a dogfight and did not return to his base. Later the wreckage of his aircraft was found by the Germans, who strangely found no battle damage to Ball or his SE5a. The exact circumstances remain a mystery but no German pilot claimed this desirable victory. Captain Albert Ball, VC, DSO and two bars, MC, was credited with forty-four victories and

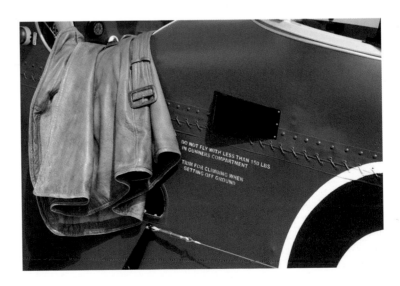

Aircraft were so light that even the smallest change in weight distribution could upset the balance (see the written warning on the fuselage).

DO NOT FLY WITH LESS THAN 150 LBS
IN GUNNERS COMPARTMENT
TRIM FOR CLIMBING WHEN
GETTING OFF GROUND

died a few months short of his twenty-first birthday. Like McCudden he was a 'stalker' who preferred to use altitude and the sun to gain the ideal position to swoop down and attack an unsuspecting foe from behind and below (von Richthofen employed similar tactics).

Cockpit instrumentation was basic in the extreme, and disorientation common. Lieutenant F. H. Thayre, based in Merville, France, with No. 16 Squadron flying a BE2a loaded with two 112-lb bombs, became lost in a snowstorm. Finding himself over water, he deduced that

A German Albatros DV fighter.

The Ripping Panel (Issue No. 2, March 1918), the in-house magazine produced at RNAS Polegate in Sussex. A ripping panel was a patch on the side of an airship which could be easily ripped away in dire straits, allowing a rapid escape of gas and descent.

41

the nearest land was Holland. With petrol exhausted, he landed at Sheerness, Kent, and allegedly surrendered to the first person he encountered – the confused local could not understand why a British pilot wanted to surrender to anyone in Kent. After depositing his bombs at RNAS Westgate, he hopped around Kent, returning to his La Gorge airfield five days late. His colleagues sympathetically composed a ditty in his honour:

> There was a young pilot called Thayre
> Who fancied a trip in the air
> When his petrol was spent
> He landed in Kent
> And surrendered at once to the Mayor!

A crashed Sopwith Camel of No. 203 Squadron. The inherent instability of the Camel made it an excellent fighter but potentially dangerous for a novice to fly. Half of those built were lost in take-off or landing accidents. (IWM Q 12121)

Captain Thayre was killed in June 1917 by 'Archie' while flying an FE2d with No. 20 Squadron. He is credited with twenty victories and held the MC and bar.

In his largely autobiographical novel *Winged Victory* V. M. Yeates, who flew Sopwith Camels during 1918, mainly on highly dangerous ground-strafing missions, has the main character struggling with battle fatigue but declining an easy escape for fear of being seen to be afraid. Most post-war literature emerged from the pens of pilots and, in the main, from Scout pilots. Many admitted to their fears and in particular that of fire in the air. In an age before armour-plate protection and parachutes (balloon crews used these, as did the Germans towards the end) the prospect of falling several thousand feet soaked in petrol in a burning aeroplane was literally the stuff of nightmares. The hero of Yeates's novel was eventually observed by the wing medical officer and sent home, classified 'flying sickness D' (for debility), given one month leave and posted to home establishment second-line duties. Captain Yeates of No. 46 Squadron, who had five victories to his name, survived the war but with broken health. He died aged thirty-four.

It is commonly held that parachutes were not issued because callous senior officers thought that pilots would abandon their aeroplanes whilst there was a chance of saving a valuable machine. Obviously senior officers had no experience of aerial combat and some may have felt this but the fact is that the early machines were barely able to carry a crew and weapons/camera and would not have been able to manage the extra weight of the primitive parachutes. In July 1917 the RNAS authorised one parachute per airship, which must have led to interesting conversations when things went awry! The RAF placed an order for five hundred parachutes in September 1918 but none were used during the war. Interestingly, even into the 1920s many pilots declined them. Arthur Gould Lee, with No. 46 Squadron flying Sopwith Pups, recalled his horror in June 1917:

> I keep thinking of the flames today. The pilot jumped. He had a light yellow coat and it bellied out, momentarily checking his fall like a parachute so that the machine left him behind ... What a way to die, to be sizzled alive or to jump and fall thousands of feet ...

The future of naval flying: Squadron Commander E. H. Dunning successfully landed a Sopwith Pup on HMS *Furious* on 2 August 1917. Although he was tragically killed on his third attempt, naval warfare would never be the same again. (IWM Q 20637)

Millions may have died but that did not lessen the loss felt by an individual. The mother of Captain Francis Mond searched for her 'missing' son, viewing remains and opening graves, until she achieved success in 1923. Her son and his observer now have named headstones. The family purchased the area immediately surrounding the crash site at Bouzencourt, on the Somme, and erected this memorial.

Edward 'Mick' Mannock had a pathological fear of death, especially by fire, and habitually carried a pistol to use in preference to being burnt alive. Although regarded as a slow starter in danger of being labelled 'yellow', he proved the most successful British pilot of the war. His total number of victories is still debated. He was a great teacher who coached novices to survive and would let one finish and claim a victory of which he had already made certain. A great German-hater, he would rejoice over a flaming victim and shoot up any crashed airman on the ground who showed signs of life. Chivalrous? Von Richthofen did the same!

Largely unknown to the public, on 26 July 1918 he was shot down by ground fire in the flames that he dreaded after breaking his own rule never to follow a doomed enemy down. His grave was lost in subsequent fighting and he is remembered on the Arras Flying Services Memorial, which commemorates airmen with no known burial site. In July 1919 Major Edward Mannock was awarded the posthumous VC to add to the DSO and bar and MC and bar. He had been profoundly affected when McCudden died on 9 July 1918.

Major James McCudden, VC, DSO and bar, MC and bar, MM, was flying from England to take command of No. 60 Squadron when he landed at Auxi-le-Château airfield for directions. Taking off again, his engine failed owing to an incorrect carburettor having been fitted. The total airman – pilot, instructor, tactician, mechanic, rigger and crack shot – died and was buried in Wavans Cemetery. Before parting from his sister to fly to France he handed her an envelope. It contained his medals. Not only his elder but also his younger brother were killed flying with the RFC.

An affable, charismatic man, McCudden had grown short-tempered and had begun to take risks that he would never have contemplated earlier. He had used his mechanical skills to make his personal SE5a the fastest on the Front, able to climb to about 20,000 feet where the temperature was minus thirty degrees centigrade, where oxygen would now be mandatory. On landing he would go through agony as he thawed out and suffered blinding headaches from anoxia. When stalking a Rumpler reconnaissance aeroplane at 21,000 feet he discovered that part of his Vickers machine gun had broken into pieces and that his Lewis had seized up as a result of the extreme cold.

After the war much was made of the scores of the Aces. Not all claims stand the test of post-war research but they were almost always made in good faith. Trenchard insisted that the RFC have their own 'front line' on the far side of the front line on the ground. The majority of the fighting therefore occurred over German-held territory, where it was not possible to verify claims by visiting the crash sites. Each participating country had their own yardstick regarding victories. The British awarded victories for definitely destroying an aircraft or balloon, and also for sending one down 'out of control' or 'forcing one down'. In the latter cases a canny pilot might spin down from a losing fight, recover at low level and live to fight another day. Efforts were made to seek independent verification from the ground and combat reports had to be submitted from squadron to wing to headquarters before claims were confirmed and medals awarded.

The Flying Services Memorial at Arras, Somme, to British airmen lost on the Western Front who have no known grave, contains nearly one thousand names.

AROUND THE WORLD

Aʟᴛʜᴏᴜɢʜ the First World War is, for many, synonymous with the Western Front, airmen fought in Palestine, Mesopotamia, Salonika, Africa, Italy and Russia. Airmen also fought over the North Sea and the Mediterranean, where they flew from the world's first aircraft carriers. Each campaign had particular problems, and even unique achievements. In April 1916 No. 30 Squadron was called on to help the besieged garrison of Kut El Amara in Mesopotamia, in modern-day Iraq. In two weeks they dropped some fourteen tons of food, medical supplies and ammunition in the world's first attempt at air supply, although the garrison was eventually forced to surrender. Worldwide, British airmen improvised and overcame, but events far away were frequently overshadowed by more immediate news on the home and western fronts.

The Australian Flying Corps (AFC) was formed in 1912 with a Central Flying School at Point Cook in Victoria. At the outbreak of war Australia sent aircraft to capture the German colony in New Guinea but the Germans capitulated before the aircraft were unpacked. It was in the desert that No. 1 Squadron AFC was bloodied with action in Palestine. By 1918 they were equipped with Bristol Fighters and did great work in support of the Australian Light Horse and British Yeomanry mounted columns. Apart from dealing with the Turkish enemy, they and the British had disease, flies, heat, sand, lack of water and sometimes shortage of food to contend with, together with hostile Arabs. About this time, after several downed crews were killed by Arabs or handed to the Turks, 'goolie chits' were issued — 'blood chits' to the more sensitive. These offered a bounty for the return of the bearer into British hands, subject to his being in a complete condition!

On 21 September 1918 No. 1 Squadron AFC joined three British squadrons in the near total annihilation of the 7th Turkish Army, about half the Turkish strength in Palestine, in a terrible exhibition of the potential of airpower. The Turks were retreating through the Wadi el Fara valley when attacking aircraft blocked both ends. Bristol Fighters of No. 1 Squadron AFC flew multiple sorties, supported by No. 144 Squadron RAF flying DH9 bombers and Nos. 111 and 145 Squadrons RAF with SE5a fighters also carrying bombs. No one counted the dead but about one hundred guns and over a thousand vehicles were destroyed. Two aeroplanes were shot down but one crew was rescued by the pursuing Australian Light Horsemen. Some 9.25 tons of bombs were dropped and 56,000 rounds of ammunition fired. Many pilots admitted to feeling physically sick at the slaughter. The Turks requested an Armistice on 31 October.

The only Australian air VC was awarded to Lieutenant Frank McNamara, an ex-schoolteacher, who joined No. 1 Squadron AFC in December 1916. On 20 March 1917 he was flying in a Martinsyde G100 Scout carrying bombs and also acting as escort to two BE2s tasked to bomb a section of railway. McNamara was injured in his leg by the premature explosion of one of his bombs but he landed under fire to rescue the pilot of a downed BE2. On taking off with the other pilot clinging to the wing he lost control owing to his wounded leg and crashed. They went back to the downed machine and, despite the damage, he flew them to safety.

Most aerial opposition was flown by Germans. Several Australian pilots scored seven victories in Palestine including Lieutenant P. J. 'Ginty' McGuiness who, after the war, joined his observer Lieutenant W. H. Fysh in forming the Qantas airline.

Following pages: No. 201 Squadron in France in August 1918, displaying the variety of uniforms typical of the early months of the RAF. (IWM CO 2858)

Powerful engine torque made the very responsive Sopwith Camel potentially lethal to a novice and equally lethal to the Germans in the hands of an experienced pilot. The rotary engine could bear a greater degree of punishment than water-cooled engines and led to Camels flying dangerous low-level strafing missions.

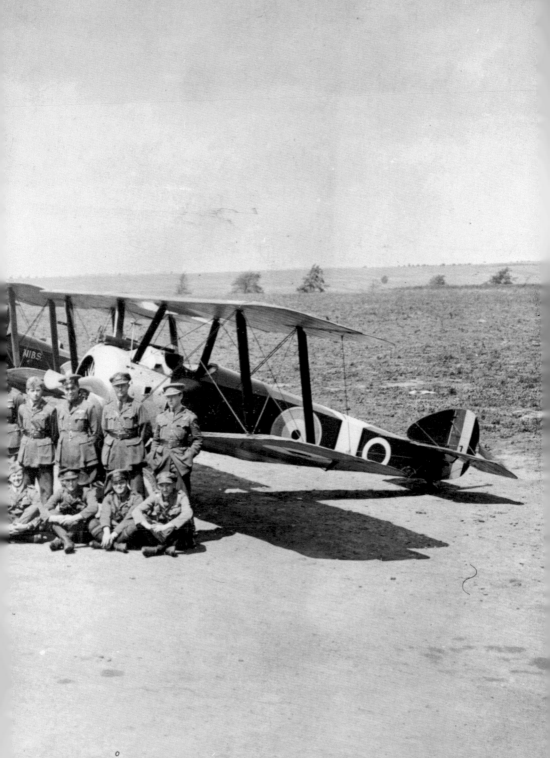

Another notable Australian from the desert was Captain Ross 'Hadji' Smith who not only shot down eleven enemy machines but took over a Handley Page 0/400 bomber sent to Palestine at the behest of Lieutenant Colonel T. E. Lawrence ('of Arabia', who later served in the RAF as Aircraftsman Shaw). After flying a large quantity of fuel and ammunition to Lawrence during the Battle of Nablus he bombed the Turkish headquarters and the El Afule telephone exchange wiping out all Turkish communications. On 12 November 1919 he joined his brother Keith to achieve a world's first by flying from Hounslow, London, to Darwin, Australia, in a converted Vimy bomber, arriving on 10 December. They were knighted but he died in a flying accident on 14 April 1922.

Dunkirk aerodrome from the air. The aircraft are believed to be No. 3 Squadron 'Fees'. (IWM Q 11552)

Three other Australian squadrons fought on the Western Front and additionally other Australians flew with British squadrons. It is believed that eighty-one Australians reached 'Ace' status. Major R. A. Little, who was the most successful with forty-seven victories, flew with No. 8 (Naval) Squadron and No. 203 Squadron RAF. Altogether 460 officers and 2,234 from other ranks served in the AFC. Another two hundred served as aircrew with the British squadrons. A total of 175 were killed, 111 were wounded, 6 were gassed and 40 became prisoners of war.

Men of other Empire countries also volunteered to fly with the British. This is perhaps not surprising as many were the sons or grandsons of British emigrants and quite possibly regarded themselves as British. Canada provided 20,000 volunteers and in 1917 the RFC established training schools in Canada. Three Canadians were honoured with the VC. Two were Scout Aces: Lieutenant Colonel William 'Billy' Bishop and Major W. G. Barker. The third, Second Lieutenant Alan 'Babe' McLeod, trained in Canada before joining No. 2 Squadron flying the Armstrong Whitworth FK8 'Big Ack'. On 27 March 1918 he was attempting to bomb a balloon site in foul weather when he spotted a German Triplane Scout. It was shot down by his observer, Lieutenant A. W. Hammond, whereupon eight more Triplanes attacked. Hammond shot down another two but both men were wounded and their 'bus' was badly shot about. As it burst into flames, the cockpit floor burnt away. Hammond climbed onto the rear fuselage and McLeod onto the left wing, holding the control column and side-slipping to keep the flames away from the machine. One enemy stayed to watch and Hammond shot him down. McLeod crash landed in No Man's Land and crawled with Hammond on his back into the British trenches. After hospitalisation he returned to Canada but died of influenza, aged nineteen years.

New Zealand also provided men and opened two flying schools. Fifteen New Zealanders became Aces, led by Major Keith 'Grid' Caldwell with twenty-five victories. The second was a man synonymous with Britain's 'finest hour' — Major Keith Park whose tactics as Air Vice Marshal, Commanding No. 11 Group, Fighter Command, achieved victory in the Battle of Britain. He later displayed the same skills defending Malta.

In South Africa the wounds from the Boer War may still have been raw but they had set up a flying school in Kimberley in 1912. About 3,000 served in Britain's air forces and 260 died. In the early war they were involved in attacking the German colonies in Africa but on the Western Front forty-six became 'Aces' and Captain A. F. W. Beauchamp Proctor, with fifty-four victories, won the VC.

South African Major C. J. Quintin Brand distinguished himself as a Scout pilot by day and especially by night. In 1920, together with Lieutenant Colonel H. A. 'Pierre' van Ryneveld, he flew a Vickers Vimy from London

Behold the end of a raiding " Gotha."
A prey to Kentish fire,
Our boys at the guns have finished the Huns
And lit their funeral pyre.

The end of a Gotha bomber, 22 August 1917. In this last daylight Gotha raid, three of the ten bombers were shot down, two credited to aircraft and one to anti-aircraft gunners. Henceforth they would come by night. In total, Gotha raids killed about four hundred people for the loss of thirty-two bombers.

to Cape Town, South Africa. They had to change aeroplanes twice and this disqualified them from the £10,000 prize offered by *The Times* newspaper but the South African government awarded them £5,000 each and they were knighted. In 1940 he led No. 10 Group, Fighter Command in the south-west of England and in close co-operation with A. V. M. Park the two fighter pilots worked to win victory.

Lieutenant Indra Lal 'Laddie' Roy was the only Indian Ace of the twentieth century. He joined the RFC in April 1917 and was injured as the result of a crash whilst serving with No. 56 Squadron. He recovered and joined No. 40 Squadron in June 1918, again flying the SE5a, and shot down ten of the enemy in thirteen days. He was awarded the Distinguished Flying Cross (DFC) but was killed on 22 July. He was nineteen years old.

Another Indian pilot, Lieutenant Shri Krishna Chunda Welinkar flew Sopwith Dolphins with No. 23 Squadron but died of his wounds in German hands after combat on 27 June 1918. He lies in Hangard Communal Cemetery Extension on the Somme. A third Indian pilot survived the war: Lieutenant Hardit Singh Malik flew Camels with No. 28 Squadron and was wounded in action. On leaving hospital he joined No. 141 Squadron, flying 'Biffs' from Biggin Hill, Kent, an airfield synonymous with the 'Few' in the next war. His outsized flying helmet which fitted over his turban gave him the affectionate nickname 'the Flying Hobgoblin'.

Of the nineteen VCs awarded to airmen, only one went to a sergeant pilot, Thomas Mottershead. On patrol with No. 20 Squadron on 7 July 1917, his 'Fee' was attacked by two Albatros fighters and the fuel tank directly behind him was set alight. Rather than land in German territory he flew on whilst his observer, Lieutenant W. E. Gower, sprayed a fire extinguisher over him. When he finally landed the undercarriage collapsed, throwing Gower clear but trapping Mottershead. He died of his burns

four days later. Sergeant pilots were very much the victims of their times. Never very numerous, not more than thirty ever served in France at one time. Not judged suitable for commissions, they were forced to mess separately from the officer pilots, so being prevented from listening to and learning from others.

No. 141 Squadron outside the tea rooms opposite Biggin Hill aerodrome, with Lieutenant Hardit Singh Malik, affectionately known as 'the Flying Hobgoblin'.

Initially sergeants were used for second-line duties as staff pilots at observer and gunnery schools or for ferrying. Those that saw active service usually did so in two-seater squadrons. Sergeant E. J. Elton shot down ten of the enemy and his observers another six, to make him the most successful NCO pilot. Sergeant William Clarke was a black Jamaican pilot who flew RE8 'Harry Tate' two-seater reconnaissance aeroplanes with No. 4 Squadron before being injured in combat.

Sergeant Thomas Mottershead, VC, DCM. (IWM 58359)

ON THE GROUND

Drunk last night
Drunk the night before
And we're going to get drunk again tonight
If we never get drunk no more.

ALTHOUGH naval airmen afloat shared the same discomforts of seaborne life as their sailor colleagues, on-land airmen generally were better off than the rest of the fighting army. Squadrons usually stayed in the same place for months or even years at a time, and while tents were still often used, and hangars were usually only canvas, many would get to sleep in wooden huts, with proper canteens to prepare their food, messes to relax in and regular

The personal collection of an airman (with replica cloth patches). Some of the skilled mechanics made ornaments out of spare scraps of wood and metal and old bullet cases.

shifts for their work. Offices and workshops were properly built and equipped. Officers had huts with two or three to a room and a shared 'batman' (servant). There was little 'bull' in the RFC or RNAS. The men were highly competent tradesmen, often required to work long hours in poor conditions or foul weather. Greasy overalls comprised normal working wear for men highly respected by their officers, who were dependent on them for their safety.

Nor were their lives without risk. Many were killed by German night-bombing raids on their airfields, designed to cause damage and equally to disturb sleep. Major Chapman, who is commemorated in Nackington Church, and four of his mechanics, were killed in just such a raid at Popperinghe airfield.

Air Craftsman First Class John Hadaway. A skilled metal worker, he was not allowed to 'join up' until he had completed his apprenticeship in Woolwich Arsenal. Although he joined the RAF in May 1918, he was still issued with an RFC uniform.

Airfields by nature were dangerous places with spinning propellers and damaged aeroplanes landing barely under control. At Chocques aerodrome, France, in March 1915 airmen were loading a Morane aeroplane with 26-pound Melinite bombs (converted French artillery shells with a striker in the nose). Two dropped free, killing the pilot and seven airmen.

In some ways the comparative comforts of airfield life compensated for the dangers and discomforts of flying, although many airmen made full use of the entertainments available, too. Scout pilot Cecil Lewis took the following view of his flying colleagues:

> To fly in a straight line, taking photos of the enemy trenches, an easy Archie target, within range of the ground machine guns, bumped by the eddies of passing shells and pestered by enemy scouts, that required nerve. And it would have to be done twice a day, day after day, until you were hit or went home. Small wonder if, under this strain, pilots lived a wild life and wined and womanised to excess.

Alcohol played a large part in relieving pressure and was cheaply available in the officers' mess, where sing-songs and furniture-smashing party games were the norm. Downed enemy airmen would often be riotously entertained in the mess before they were led off into captivity. A British airman crashing behind German lines could expect the same treatment, while messages regarding the fate of downed airmen would often be dropped over the opposition's airfields. At times even parcels of clothing and other necessities were dropped for the comfort of colleagues who had fallen into enemy hands.

Sometimes a trip was organised to the local *estaminet* (French bar) where not only drink but female company could be found, with possibly a room out the back. Officer's home leave was regularly granted and the nightclubs, theatres and restaurants, especially in the London's West End, beckoned. Girls of all classes were in turn drawn to the young men with their wings and medals – many society ladies who would not have given a second glance at, say, Air Mechanic McCudden now vied for an introduction to Major McCudden, VC, DSO, MC, MM. Female company may have helped with morale but sometimes added to the numbers on sick parade.

Gambling was a popular recreation. The officers preferred bridge to the men's Crown and Anchor boards and it was said that wherever

A temporary airfield somewhere in France.

two Canadians met soon a poker or dice school was in full swing, usually to the financial detriment of their British friends. Sport was another option but weary men might have preferred to catch up on their sleep. The splendid Rev. 'Tubby' Clayton opened the teetotal Toc-H house in Poperinghe as an alternative refuge from war. This function was also provided by the canteens of the YMCA and the Salvation Army.

ROYAL FLYING CORPS.

RECRUITS, SKILLED or UNSKILLED

(The latter must be clerks, storemen, etc.) men of almost any occupation, are wanted for the various branches of the Royal Flying Corps.

Men of military age and UP TO FIFTY YEARS OF AGE accepted. Corps rates of pay.

Apply personally or in writing to the nearest Recruiting Officer, who will put applicants into touch with the Special Recruiting Officer of the Royal Flying Corps in this district.

Sept   GOD SAVE THE KING.   1917

An advert for mechanics dating from 1917.

The ground echelon of a squadron would consist of a reporting officer who doubled as the adjutant and intelligence officer, an equipment officer, an armament officer and an engineering officer.

Skilled non-commissioned tradesmen included blacksmiths who could use oxy-welding plant when required, coppersmiths, vulcanizers, fabric workers, carpenters, engine mechanics and airframe riggers. Each squadron had a workshop lorry to carry out machine work using electricity. They were highly trained and well paid by army standards. General Trenchard described them as follows: 'These men are the backbone of all our efforts.'

The British army had spent long periods in India and Egypt. Conversing with the locals had bred a type of Tommy-speak — English mixed with corrupted Hindi and Arabic. Now a version of corrupted French was added (see table below).

The Royal Navy, of course, retained naval terminology even when on land, while the flying services also began to develop their very own slang (see table on page 58).

Term	Translation
Bookoo	Much/plenty (*beaucoup*)
Bombadier	Potatoes (*pommes de terre*)
Bon or no bon	Good or no good (*bon*)
Comsa	What/how/why (*comme ça*)
Plonk	Wine (*vin blanc*)
San Fairy Ann	Doesn't matter (*ça ne fait rien*)
Toot sweet	Quick (*tout de suite*)
Eat apples	Etaples
Funky villas	Foncquevillers
Ocean villas	Auchonvillers
Plug Street	Ploegsteert
Wipers	Ypres

Term	Definition
Ack Emma	Airman ('AM')
Archie	Anti-aircraft artillery fire
Bounce	Attack by surprise
Breeze up	To be nervous
Bung off	Take off and go
Bus	An aircraft
Crate	An aircraft
Dogfight	An aerial fight, with aircraft swirling around each other
Hun	The enemy, be it the Germans or pupil pilots
Office	The cockpit
Sausage	An observation balloon
Split-arsed	A fast turn (from 'Split-S turn')
The Stick	Control column
Volplane	To glide down

An aircraft repair depot, 1918, where crashed or damaged aircraft could be repaired or cannibalised for parts. (IWM Q12075)

On 1 April 1918 the RNAS and RFC merged to become the Royal Air Force (RAF). It was not a universally popular move amongst the officers and other ranks, and the mixing of personnel in the previously separate squadrons was sometimes resented, but most just got on with the war. RNAS personnel in France had always worn khaki with naval caps but now they had to adjust to having army ranks for the time being. Eventually new ranks were introduced which owed much to the old RNAS ranks.

The engine repair shop, Calshot. (IWM Q 69377)

Also amalgamated on that date were the various women's organisations which became the Women's Royal Air Force (WRAF). A total strength of 90,000 was anticipated but it never exceeded 24,500. They provided not only clerical and domestic staff but also drivers, riggers, carpenters and metal workers. Some served in France and Germany after the armistice but all had been demobilised by 1920. The RAF Nursing Service was established in 1918 and treated men in Britain only. It survives today as Princess Mary's RAF Nursing Service.

On 11 November 1918 the war ended. From the acorns of the RFC and RNAS a mighty oak, the Royal Air Force, had grown.

In 1914 the strengths were as follows:
- RFC: 146 officers and 1,097 other ranks with 100 machines.
- RNAS: 130 officers and 700 other ranks with 98 machines.
- Total: 276 officers and 1,797 other ranks with 198 machines.

In 1918 members of the newly instituted Women's Royal Air Force contributed to several technical trades. (IWM 27255)

By 1918 the strengths had massively increased:
- RAF: 27,000 officers and 290,000 other ranks with 22,677 machines.

In 1918 even the aeroplanes now resembled their modern counterparts rather than a collection of wings and wires. It was said that the 1914-era Caudron G3 had approximately 120 rigging wires and was a known as 'the birdcage'. Riggers allegedly released a canary within the wings and if it escaped then more wires were added!

In his book *The Kaiser's Battle* Martin Middlebrook compares the casualty rates of subalterns in 10th Battalion West Yorkshire Regiment with those in No. 56 Squadron flying the SE5a:

	Infantry subalterns	No. 56 Squadron pilots
Killed	21.3%	41.3%
Wounded	27.6%	15.6%
Prisoner	3.4%	28.4%

The figures illustrate not only the danger of flying but that the constant aggressive posture demanded by Trenchard resulted in many men being made prisoner who could well have fought on, had they managed to force land on their own side of the front line. In addition men with wounds from which they would have recovered had they been serving on the ground were unable to survive the impact of the aeroplane hitting the ground. The case for effective parachutes speaks for itself.

The thousand names on the Arras Flying Services Memorial to the airmen of the Western Front who have no known grave emphasises the price paid.

They made courage and devotion the rule, not the exception.
Walter Raleigh, *The War in the Air*, Vol. 1

The St Omer Memorial commemorates the site of the RFC General Headquarters on arrival in France. It then became an active aerodrome and an important aircraft depot. The RFC/RAF motto 'Per Adua ad Astra' is generally held to mean 'Through Adversity to the Stars'.

FURTHER READING

Barber, Mark. *Royal Naval Air Service Pilot, 1914–18*. Osprey, 2010.

Barker, Ralph. *A Brief History of the Royal Flying Corps in World War I*. Robinson Publishing, 2002.

Bowyer, Chas. *Albert Ball, VC*. Bridge Books, revised edition, 1994.

Cole, Christopher, and Cheeseman, E. F. *The Air Defence of Britain, 1914–18*. Putnams, 1984.

Hearn, Philip. *Flying Rebel: The Story of Louis Strange*. Stationery Office Books, 1994.

Gould Lee, Arthur. *No Parachute*. Jarrolds, 1968.

Jones, Ira. *King of Air Fighters: The Biography of Major 'Mick' Mannock*. Ivor Nicholson and Watson Limited, 1935.

King, Bradley. *The Royal Naval Air Service, 1912–1918*. Hikoki Publications, 1997.

Levine, Joshua. *On a Wing and a Prayer* (reprinted in paperback in 2011 as Fighter Heroes of WW1). Collins, 2008.

Lewis, Cecil. *Sagittarius Rising*. Frontline Books, 2009.

Mackersey, Ian. *No Empty Chairs: The Short and Heroic Lives of the Young Aviators who Fought and Died in the First World War*. Weidenfeld & Nicolson, 2012.

McCudden, James. *Flying Fury: Five Years in the Royal Flying Corps*. Wrens Park, 2000.

O'Connor, Mike. *Airfields and Airmen* series. Wharncliffe Books.

Raleigh, W. A. and Jones, H. A. *The War in the Air: Being the Story of the Part Played in the Great War by the RAF*, Volumes 1–6. Naval and Military Press, 2002.

Yeates, V. M. *Winged Victory*. Grub Street, 2004.

PLACES TO VISIT

Fleet Air Arm Museum, RNAS Yeovilton, Ilchester, Somerset BA22 8HT.
   Telephone: 01935 840565. Website: www.fleetairarm.com
Imperial War Museum Duxford, Cambridgeshire CB22 4QR.
   Telephone: 01223 835000. Website: www.iwm.org.uk
Imperial War Museum London, Lambeth Road, London SE1 6HZ.
   Telephone: 020 7416 5000. Website: www.iwm.org.uk
Museum of Army Flying, Middle Wallop, Stockbridge, Hampshire SO20 8DY.
   Telephone: 01264 784421. Website: www.armyflying.com
National Museum of Flight, East Fortune Airfield, East Lothian EH39 5LF.
   Telephone: 0300 1236789. Website: www.nms.ac.uk
Royal Air Force Museum London, Grahame Park Way, London NW9 5LL.
   Telephone: 020 82052266. Website: www.rafmuseum.org.uk
The Science Museum, Exhibition Road, South Kensington, London SW7 2DD.
   Telephone: 0870 8704868. Website: www.sciencemuseum.org.uk
Shuttleworth Collection, Shuttleworth (Old Warden) Aerodrome,
   Nr. Biggleswade, Bedfordshire SG18 9EP.
   Telephone: 01767 627927. Website: www.shuttleworth.org
Stow Maries Aerodrome, Hackmans Lane, Purleigh, Nr. Maldon, Essex
   CM3 6RN.
   Telephone: 01245 808744. Website: www.stowmaries.com

SE5a Scout, one of the great Scout aircraft of the war and flown by McCudden, Mannock and Ball.

INDEX

Page numbers in italics refer to illustrations

Aircraft (British): Armstrong Whitworth FK8 51; Avro 504 *11*, 14; BE2 'Stability Jane' or 'Quirk' *11*, 20, 30–1, 33, 41, 47; Bristol F2b Fighter 'Biff' 33, *35*, *36*; Caudron G3 10, *10*; DH9 47; FE2 'Fee' *28*, *29*, 33; Felixstowe F2A/F3 25, *26*, *27*; Handley Page 0/100 and 0/400 33, 50; Handley Page V/1500 'Bloody Paralyser' 33, *33*; Martynside S1/G100 31, 47; Maurice Farman 'Longhorn' 10, *34*; Morane-Saulnier Type L Monoplane 24, *24*, 25; RE8 'Harry Tate' 53; SE5a *3*, 47, *63*; Sopwith Camel 42, *42*, *43*; Sopwith Pup *28*; Sopwith Triplane 34, *35*

Aircraft (German): Albatross D.V *41*; Eindekker 14, 29; Gotha *52*; Zeppelin 21, *21*, 23–5, *29*, 31

Airships: Airshiplane *23*; Landing 20, 21; Operational Flying 20; 'Ripping Panel' *41*

Alcock, J. 14, *34*, 40

Amiens 6

Arras Memorial *45*

Australian Light Horse/British Yeomanry 46

Australian Flying Corps 46–51

Ball, A. 11, 40

Barracks *12*

Beauchamp Proctor, A. 51

Bennett, W. G. *39*

Biggin Hill 52, *53*

Brand, C. J. Q. 51

Burke, C. J. B. 7

Calshot *59*

Canadian Airmen: 51, 57

Capel le Ferne 20

Chapman, C. *40*, 55

Chapman, W. *40*

Chatham Naval Memorial *25*

Chocques 55

Clark, W. 53

Cuxhaven 21

Dover 6

Dowding, H. 19

Dunkirk *13*

Equipment: Carrier Pigeons 25; Clothing 39, *39*; 'Goolie Chits' 46; Life jackets 25; Parachutes 17, 43, 61; Photographic equipment 18–19; Sidcot suits 39

Harvey-Kelly, H. D. 7

Henderson, Sir D. 6

Higgins, J. F. A. 7

Indian Airmen 52

Kite Balloons: Ascent *15*; Organisation 17; Training 15

Kut 46

Leefe Robinson, W. 31, *31*

Lewis, C. 55

Little, R. 51

Long Acre *30*

Lydd *19*

Mannock, E. *12*, 44

Malik, H. S. 52, *53*

McCudden, J. T. B. *Title page*, 11, 34–5, 44

McNamara, F. 47

Mond, F. 44, *44*

Morgan, L. L. 32

Motteshead, T. 52, *53*

Nabulas 50

New Zealand Airmen 51

Park, K. 51

Poperinghe 55

Rhodes-Moorehouse, W. 19

Royal Air Force: Comparison of casualties Army/Pilots 60; Merger of RFC and RNAS 59; Princess Mary's RASF Nursing Service 59; Repair Depot *58*; Strength in 1918; WRAF 59, *60*

Royal Flying Corps: Formation 5; Central Flying School 9; Clock Code 18; Gosport System 14–15; Strength in 1914 59

Royal Naval Air Service: Attacks on Zeppelin sheds 7; Eastchurch NFS 9; Seaplane Carriers 6, 21–3, *23*, *26*; Spiders Web Strength in 1914 59; Uniforms *4*

Roy, I. 52

Samson, C. 6, *6*

Slang 57–8

Smith-Barry, R. 14

South African Airmen 51–2

Squadrons: No.2 6–7; No.3 6; No.4 6, 53; No.5 6, 7; No.16 41–2; No.29 13; No.30 46; No.39 (Home Defence) 32; No.46 42–3; No.50 (Home Defence) 32; No.111 47; No.111 52, No.144 47; No.145 47; No.201 *48*; No. 9 (Reserve) 11; No.1 A.F.C. 46

St Omer 61, *61*

Stow Maries 30, *32*

Strange, L. 7, 11, 29

Sueter, M. 6

Thayre, F. 41–2

Toc H 57

Trenchard, H. 14, 44, 57

Usborne, N. 23, *23*

Victoria Cross awards 19, 40, 44, 47, 51, 52

Wadi el Fara 46

Warneford, R. 13, 24, *24*, 25

West Indian Pilot 53

Yeates, V. 42